Sadie

David Ireland

methuen | drama

LONDON • NEW YORK • OXFORD • NEW DELHI • SYDNEY

METHUEN DRAMA
Bloomsbury Publishing Plc
50 Bedford Square, London, WC1B 3DP, UK
1385 Broadway, New York, NY 10018, USA
29 Earlsfort Terrace, Dublin 2, Ireland

BLOOMSBURY, METHUEN DRAMA and the Methuen Drama logo are
trademarks of Bloomsbury Publishing Plc

First published in Great Britain 2021

A catalogue record for this book is available from the British Library.

ISBN: PB: 978-1-3502-5657-6
ePDF: 978-1-3502-5658-3
eBook: 978-1-3502-5659-0

Series: Modern Plays

Typeset by Mark Heslington Ltd, Scarborough, North Yorkshire

To find out more about our authors and books visit
www.bloomsbury.com and sign up for our newsletters.

Sadie

by David Ireland

Belfast
City Council

arts
council
of Northern Ireland

LOTTERY FUNDED

David is from Belfast and trained as an actor at the RSAMD (now Royal Conservatoire of Scotland).

His plays include *What the Animals Say* (Oran Mor, Glasgow), *Everything Between Us* (Tinderbox, Belfast), *The End of Hope* (Oran Mor, Glasgow), *Yes So I Said Yes* (Ransom, Belfast), *Can't Forget About You* (Lyric, Belfast), *Cyprus Avenue* (Abbey, Dublin/Royal Court, London/Public, NYC) and *Ulster American* (Traverse, Edinburgh). He adapted Lorca's *Blood Wedding* for Dundee Rep and Graeae.

He was Playwright-in-Residence at the Lyric Theatre, Belfast 2011–2012. He won the Stewart Parker Award and the Meyer Whitworth Award in 2012 for *Everything Between Us* and was shortlisted for the Evening Standard Award for Most Promising Playwright 2016 for *Cyprus Avenue*. *Cyprus Avenue* also won the Irish Times Award for Best New Play and the James Tait Black Award in 2017. In 2018, *Ulster American* won the Carol Tambor Best of Edinburgh Award, a Scotsman Fringe First and the Critics Award for Theatre in Scotland for Best New Play.

He has written several radio plays and, for television, two episodes of *The Young Offenders* (RTE/BBC). He has a TV series in development with Sky Atlantic and is also writing a new play for Sonia Friedman Productions.

The Lyric Theatre

The Lyric Theatre is a playhouse for all. We are a shared civic space for artists and audiences alike; a creative hub for theatre-making and nurturing talent. Our mission is to create, entertain, and inspire.

Over the past seventy years, the Lyric has established itself as Northern Ireland's leading producing theatre, premiering the works of playwrights such as Stewart Parker, Owen McCafferty, Martin Lynch, Marie Jones, David Ireland, Abbie Spallen and Christina Reid, and showcasing the talents of Northern Ireland's finest actors, including Adrian Dunbar, Conleth Hill, Stella McCusker, Ciarán Hinds, Roma Tomelty, Tara-Lynne O'Neill, Kerri Quinn and the Theatre's Patron Liam Neeson.

With the establishment of the Lyric's New Writing department in 2016 has come a renewed vigour to seek out and support the most exciting new and emerging artists. Through our New Playwrights Programme we have developed the work of the next generation's most promising rising talents.

David Ireland was the Lyric Theatre's Artist-in-Residence in 2011–12. The Lyric produced *Can't Forget About You* in 2014 and again in 2015, in a revival co-produced with Tron Theatre. The Lyric presented *Ulster American* in a Traverse Theatre Company production in 2019. His short film *Love Lockdown* was commissioned and produced by the Lyric Theatre in partnership with BBC Arts and BBC Northern Ireland as part of their *Splendid Isolation* series, which was filmed and broadcast during the first NI Covid-19 lockdown in June 2020.

Sadie was rehearsed and filmed in January to March 2021, during the third NI Covid-19 lockdown and in compliance with government guidelines. It was filmed on the Main Stage of the Lyric Theatre for BBC Arts and BBC NI.

Sadie was first produced by the Lyric Theatre, in association with Field Day Theatre Company for BBC Arts.

The Lyric Theatre is supported by the Arts Council of Northern Ireland and Belfast City Council.

Field Day Theatre Company

Field Day Theatre Company began in 1980 in Derry as a cultural and intellectual response to the troubles in the North of Ireland. Playwright Brian Friel and actor/director Stephen Rea set out to identify and develop a new audience for theatre. Friel's critically acclaimed *Translations* was the first of many Field Day plays to show at Derry's Guildhall before travelling throughout Ireland and the world. *Sadie* was originally commissioned by Field Day Theatre Company.

Cast

Sadie	**Abigail McGibbon**
Red	**Patrick Jenkins**
Clark	**David Pearse**
Joao	**Santino Smith**
Mairead	**Andrea Irvine**

Creative Team

Writer	David Ireland
Director	Conleth Hill
Assistant Director	Seón Simpson
Set Designer	Stuart Marshall
Lighting Designer	Paul Keogan
Sound Designer	Chris Warner
Costume Designer	Gillian Lennox & Erin Charteris
Voice Director	Patricia Logue
Fight Director	Lemuel Black

Lyric Production Team

Executive Producer	Jimmy Fay
Producer	Bronagh McFeely
Casting Director	Clare Gault
Literary Manager	Rebecca Mairs
Head of Production	Adrian Mullan
Head of Finance	Micheál Meegan
Head of Marketing	Claire Murray
Marketing Manager	Rachel Leitch
Company Stage Manager	Siobhán Barbour
Deputy Stage Manager	Louise Bryans
Assistant Stage Manager	Seána Green
	Stephen Dix
Costume Supervisor	Gillian Lennox
Costume Assistant	Erin Charteris
Production Assistant	Kerry Fitzsimmons
Senior Techncian	Ian Vennard

Technicans	Corentin West
	Patrick Freeman
	Annemarie Langan
Chief LX	Jonny Daley
LX Programmer	Conal Clapper

The Lyric

Creative Learning Manager	Pauline McKay
Creative Learning Schools Co-Ordinator	Erin Hoey
Creative Learning Intern	Mark Mcilhagga
Head Of Customer Service	Julie McKegney
Duty Supervisors	Hannah Conlon
Box Office Supervisor	Emily White
Box Office Deputy Supervisor	Paul McCaffrey
Box Office Deputy Supervisor (Maternity Cover)	Donal Morgan
Housekeeping	Debbie Duff
	Amanda Richards
	Samantha Walker
Customer Service Staff	Pamela Armstrong
	Shireen Azarmi
	Luke Bannon
	Carla Bryson
	Hannah Conlon
	Ellison Craig
	Alacoque Davey
	Ryan Donnelly
	Scott English
	Thomas Finnegan
	Ella Griffin
	Marina Hampton
	Holly Hannaway
	Desmond Havlin
	Cathal Henry
	Teresa Hill
	Lauren Hutchinson
	Gerard Kelly
	Fergal Lindsay
	Caitlin Magnall-Kearns
	Laura McAleenan
	Patricia McGreevy
	Suke McKegney
	Mary McManus
	Ronan McManus

	Cathan McRoberts
	Catherine Moore
	Samantha Obman
	Bernadette Owens
	Bobbi Rai Purdy
	Caelan Stow
	Thomas Wells
Casual Technicans	Ryan Bentley
	Conal Clapper
	Damien Cox
	Jonny Daley
	Patrick Freeman
	Phelan Hardy
	Ciaran Kelly
	Annemarie Langan
	Barry McCusker
	Shelia Murphy
	Matt Rice
	Michael Stapleton
Volunteers	Jean Dumas
	Yvonne Dumas
	Joan Gormley
	Eveline Wilkinson

Acknowledgements

Thanks to the following people for reading the play and offering advice and encouragement:

Gabriel Quigley, Kirsty Williams, Frances Poet, Lisa Foster, Erica Murray, Max Elton, Vicky Featherstone, DC Jackson.

Endless thanks to my wife Jennifer, for all her love and support.

Sincere thanks to:

Cara Kelly, Peter Kelly, Ewan Donald, Fiona Sturgeon Shea and everyone at Playwrights' Studio Scotland for their help with the development of the play.

Jessica Sykes and Georgia Kanner at Independent Talent.

Jimmy Fay, Rebecca Mairs and everyone at the Lyric – still my favourite theatre in the world.

Dom O'Hanlon and everyone at Methuen Drama.

Special thanks to Abigail McGibbon and Conleth Hill for helping me discover Sadie's voice.

And above all else, thanks to Stephen Rea, for keeping faith with the play for so long. It wouldn't exist without him.

David Ireland

Sadie

For Elijah

Characters

Sadie, *fifties*
Red, *Sadie's uncle, sixties*
Clark, *Sadie's ex-husband, forties*
Joao, *Sadie's boyfriend, twenties*
Mairead, *Sadie's therapist, fifties*

Scene One

Sadie *stands alone on stage.*

Sadie   Where to begin . . .

We could start with my uncle, I suppose.

Red *appears.*

Red   Hello!

Sadie   Oh, you're here?

Red   I'm here!

Sadie   His name was Red.

Red   Not my real name.

Sadie   Why did they call you Red?

Red   I was a communist. A big union man. Forever fighting on behalf of the little fella.

Sadie   I don't know why I remember you like this. This isn't how you really were.

Red   What do you mean?

Sadie   You were never this avuncular.

Red   Am I not normally avuncular? I feel very avuncular.

Sadie   But you're not here.

Red   I'm not what?

Sadie   Well, you're not really here now. You're in my imagination.

Red   How do you mean?

Sadie   You exist only in my imagination. You're not real.

Red   I'm not *real*?

Sadie   No. You're dead. You died about thirty years ago.

Red   Fuck off.

Sadie   It's true.

Red   What year is this?

Sadie   2020.

Red   2020?!

Sadie   That's what I said.

Red   But that's the future!

Sadie   It's the present now.

Red   What's it like in 2020? Is there robots?

Sadie   No. Well, actually there are robots. But they're not very advanced. Everything's done on computers now. Computers have taken over our lives. And mobile phones. That's probably the thing you'd notice first if you were really here. Everybody looking at their tiny wee phones.

Red   Aye I could see that coming. With the 'yuppies' and that.

Sadie   You'd hate it.

Red   So what else is new?

Sadie   What else can I tell you . . .

Red   I take it Ireland is finally united?

Sadie   No way. And it never will be. But there's peace.

Red   There's peace?

Sadie   That's right.

Red   The boys put down their guns, did they?

Sadie   They did.

Red   And your lot too?

Sadie   Indeed.

Red   And what of that terrible man Paisley?

Sadie   He's dead now.

Red   Good! I mean not good. You should never wish a man dead but . . . no fuck it, I'm glad he's dead. I hated that aul' bastard

Sadie   Before that he was first minister.

Red   What does that mean?

Sadie   He was, the . . . 'prime minister'. Of Northern Ireland.

Red   I don't believe you.

Sadie   He was.

Red   But how could the good Catholic people of this country sleep in peace with that monster at the helm? Who could hope to keep such a tyrant in check?

Sadie   Martin McGuinness.

Red   Sorry, what?

Sadie   Martin McGuinness was joint first minister alongside him.

Red   What the hell are you talking about?

Sadie   They sat in government together sharing power. And they became best of pals. People called them the Chuckle Brothers because they laughed at each other's jokes so much.

Red   This sounds made up.

Sadie   I swear on your grave.

Red   Well, I take back everything I said about him. If he was pals with Martin he couldn't have been all bad.

But does this mean Ireland is still under the brutal yoke of John Bull?

Sadie   Still part of the UK, yes.

Red   The Brits are still there?

Sadie   The army is gone. There's a devolved assembly where we all share power. At least, that's the theory.

Red   How can that keep both sides happy?

Sadie   Nationalists think it's a stepping stone to a united Ireland. Unionists think it secures the union with Britain. Both are wrong. And both are right. It was going well for a while but then there was Brexit.

Red   *Brexit*? What's that? It sounds awful.

Sadie   It's Britain leaving Europe.

Red   Ahhhh now. I could see that coming. The Brits never liked Europe. They always thought they were better than the French and the Germans. Sure they think they're better than everyone.

Sadie   You were never so perspicacious while you lived.

Red   'Perspicacious'. That's a fine word. But I don't like this word Brexit. That's an ugly word.

Sadie   It's a portmanteau.

Red   'Portmanteau'! And that's a fine word too. What does it mean?

Sadie   A portmanteau is a combination of two separate words into a new word.

Red   So of which two existing words is the portmanteau 'Brexit' derived?

Sadie   'British' and 'exit'.

Red   So Brexit is a 'British exit'?

Sadie   Exactly.

Red   Well, I like the sound of a 'British exit' but it's not Europe they should be leaving, it's fucking Ireland! They should have Brexited the fuck out of this country centuries ago.

Sadie   Oi you! Remember I'm British!

Red   Ack you only think you're British. I'm talking about the real Brits.

Sadie   Well, many people worry that Brexit will endanger the peace.

Red   Well, it's great there's peace to endanger in the first place. Well done everyone. For making that happen. I'm only sorry I wasn't around to see it. So when did I die?

Sadie   1992.

Red   Was it a heart attack?

Sadie   It was.

Red   Aye, it's all coming back to me now. Was I watching *Cheers*?

Sadie   You were.

Red   God I used to love *Cheers*. Here, did Sam and Diane ever get together? Or did he end up with Rebecca?

Sadie   If I remember correctly, he ended up alone.

Red   Aye, I could see that coming. Typical Sam Malone, he was a hard one for the women to tie down. A bit like myself in that regard.

So I never recovered from that heart attack. I remember it coming and telling myself. 'Och, you'll be alright, Red. You'll be fine.'

Sadie   You were wrong.

Red   That was it then . . . the end.

Sadie   I'm afraid so.

Red   Was there many at the funeral?

Sadie   There were a good few.

Red   How many?

Sadie   Twenty or thirty.

Red   Christ.

Sadie   Closer to thirty.

Red   I would have hoped for more.

Sadie   Thirty's not bad now.

Red   Was Aoife O'Sullivan there?

Sadie   Who was Aoife O'Sullivan?

Red   You'd remember Aoife O'Sullivan. She'd only the one arm. I loved her but I thought I could do better. I didn't fancy getting half a hug at bedtime every night. And then your mother's sister came along and I settled.

Sadie   Auntie Annie.

Red   Your Auntie Annie. A fine woman with all her limbs intact. But she was no Aoife O'Sullivan. And a black-hearted Protestant bitch she was too, God rest her soul.

Sadie   I have to forgive my uncle his casual sectarianism. My family, all Sandy Row loyalists, didn't exactly welcome the news that Auntie Annie had fallen for a West Belfast Catholic.

Red   It was just a one-night thing but she got in the family way.

Sadie   I only found this out recently.

Red   So we got married. And then we lost the baby. We never had another.

You went then? To my funeral?

Sadie   Of course.

Red   Thank you.

Sadie   You were always kind to me. You made me believe I could make something of myself.

Red   You were a clever wee girl. Good with the words. A storyteller! You could have been a great novelist, another Edna O'Brien!

Sadie   Ak, away!

Red   And you were some singer too. What a singing voice this girl had.

Sadie   Aye, you taught me all the rebel songs. Got me in some trouble when I was wee. Singing 'Come Out Ye Black and Tans' outside the Rangers bar on Sandy Row.

Red   Well, l always told you never to sing them to anyone else! It was our wee secret!

Sadie   I was only a girl!

Red   And did you ever become a singer?

Sadie   No no.

Red   Did you become a novelist then?

Sadie   No.

Red   So what did you end up doing?

Sadie   I'm a cleaner.

Red   Oh . . . that's right, I remember now.

Sure there's no shame in cleaning. You have to feed the little ones.

Sadie   Never had any little ones. Clark and I divorced not long after you died. I never met anyone else.

Red   Ack, Sadie.

Sadie   It's ok. I'm happy.

Red   Well, that's the main thing. Kids are a curse anyway. I could never stand them.

Sadie   Aye . . . aye . . .

Red   Will you sing for us now?

Sadie   No!

Red   Ah go on, Sadie! A good Irish song!

Sadie   I haven't sang this long time.

Red   I remember when you were six or seven you would sit on my knee and sing 'Carrickfergus'. (*He sings.*)

   I wish I had you in Carrickfergus.

What a voice this girl had! What a talent you were!

Sadie   I remember too.

Ok.

You can go now.

Red   But is there nothing else I need to know? Tell me more about 2020.

Sadie   It's been a terrible year. Believe me, you don't want to know more. I haven't even mentioned Covid-19.

Red   Oh God, is that one of those awful bands you listen to? Like Level 42? Heaven 17? I hate all that racket.

Sadie   Covid-19's a disease. Everyone's wearing masks.

Red   Oh God, will I get it?

Sadie   You're already dead.

Red   You can't be too careful.

Sadie   I don't have time for this. You have to go.

Red   Fine.

He is about to leave when another man enters. This is **Clark**.

Clark   Is it my bit yet?

Sadie   No.

Clark   It's just I was gonna make myself a cup of tea and I wasn't sure if there was time.

Red   Who's that there? Is that aul' Clark McIlvenney I see?

Clark   Who's this now?

Red   It's Red! It's aul' Red Donaghy from Ballymurphy!

Clark   Holy Christ, is that you Red? What are you up to these days?

Red   Well, it turns out I'm dead.

Clark   You are not! What happened?

Red   Heart attack.

Clark   You're kidding.

Red   I was watching *Cheers*.

Sadie   Could you two continue this elsewhere please?

Red   Sorry, Sadie!

Clark   Sorry, love!

They exit.

Sadie   That's Clark. My ex-husband. Also dead now. Him and Red were inseparable. Despite the fact that Clark was a die-hard anti-Catholic bigot.

And I was lying to my uncle about the heart attack. He was murdered by the UVF. But I didn't want to remind him.

I should say though that despite what you've heard so far this isn't a story about the Troubles.

If anything this is what you might call a romantic comedy.

Scene Two

Sadie   I think I'm in love.

And I don't fall in love lightly.

I hate love.

It's a curse

It destroys everything.

Better to hate.

I hate everything.

I've always hated everything but I've got worse in middle age.

I hate 2020.

I hate everyone younger than me.

I hate the lockdown.

I hate masks.

I hate Twitter.

I hate snowflakes.

I hate memes.

I hate gifs.

I hate that everyone has to have a fucking opinion about everything these days.

I hate that everyone's so easily fucking offended.

I hate Netflix and all the endless fucking channels now.

I hate the new normal.

Every time I hear that phrase I want to fucking boak.

Fuck the new normal.

I miss the old normal.

I miss the old days.

I can't even believe I'm calling them that.

It doesn't feel that long ago.

The nineties.

The eighties.

The seventies.

I miss *Fawlty Towers*.

I miss *The Cosby Show*.

I miss *Buffy*.

I miss *Roseanne*.

I miss *Cheers*.

I miss staying up late with my uncle watching black and white movies.

I miss Lauren Bacall and Bette Davis.

I miss Robert Mitchum and Jimmy Cagney.

I miss Van Halen and Def Leppard.

I miss having a slim waist.

I miss Thatcher and Reagan.

I miss Bill Clinton and Tony Blair.

Because even though they were cunts at least it felt like they were grown-ups and they knew what they were doing, even if what they were doing was shit.

I miss my mother.

I hate that I've inherited her sickening addiction to nostalgia. Running around in the eighties with her beehive hairdo, moaning about how my music couldn't compare to Tommy Steele and Adam Faith.

Well, now I'm worse than her.

I miss everything.

I miss my childhood.

And I want it back.

Joao *enters.*

Sadie   I wonder what my mother would have thought of him.

Joao.

That's his name.

It's impossible to pronounce.

He's Portuguese.

(Well, English but his parents are Portuguese.)

And yes he is young but don't judge me.

Isn't it funny the times we live in people are more disgusted by age gaps in relationships than anything else?

We always have to be disgusted by something.

He's twenty-six.

Joao   I'm twenty-five.

Sadie   He's a student at Queen's but he works as a temp at the place that I clean.

Joao   It's an insurance company in Belfast city centre, I don't know if we can name them.

Sadie   Axa.

Joao   It's Axa.

Sadie   He's fucking gorgeous.

Joao   I'm not gorgeous.

Sadie   And he's so nice. Why are you so nice?

Joao   I don't think I'm that nice –

Sadie   You are!

Joao   I just think life is hard for everyone. So why be a dick?

Sadie   Do you know what I like most about you?

Joao   What?

Sadie   Your eyebrows.

Joao *raises his eyebrows suggestively. They both laugh.*

Joao   You know what I like most about you?

Sadie   What?

He whispers in her ear. She dissolves into a fit of giggles, so does he. She slaps him playfully.

Sadie   Stop it, stop it!

They compose themselves.

Usually the office temps and the cleaners don't talk to each other. But he talked to me.

Joao   I always used to pass her and I thought she was really hot, you know I've always been into the whole MILF thing? If you check my browsing history on Pornhub that's all you'll see – MILF POV, MILF PMV, lesbian MILFS wrestling.

Sadie   Jesus!

Joao   But I'm not an idiot, I know that life isn't like porn and in my experience most older women don't really like younger men or if they do they're not prepared to act on it. Like, I don't know, maybe they're more self-conscious about their bodies or maybe they have more sensitivity to a young guy's feelings, whereas a fifty-year-old-man will fuck a twenty-year-old-girl without a second thought.

Sadie   That's true.

Joao   But anyway I was too scared to talk to Sadie cos she is quite intimidating if you don't know her. But one day, I was struggling with the code for the door, so I asked for her help.

Sorry, do you know the –

Sadie   And I told him.

1690.

He punches it in.

Joao   That doesn't work.

Sadie   It's not really 1690, that was a joke.

Joao *looks confused.*

Sadie   King Billy? The Battle of the Boyne?

Joao   Sorry, I'm English.

I feel like I said that a million times my first six months in Belfast. 'Sorry, I'm English.'

Sadie   I never really noticed him before he was so quiet, but I noticed him now, in this tiny corridor pressed together. His eyes, his skin, his lips.

Where are you from?

Joao   Manchester

Sadie (*imitating him*)   'Manchester'.

Joao (*laughing*)   Shut up!

Sadie   The code is seventy-seven fourteen.

She leans across him and taps in the code. He not very subtly looks at her cleavage. She notices this.

Joao   So just those four digits.

Sadie   Four digits is usually enough I find.

Joao   I couldn't believe she said that! Did that mean what I thought it meant?

Sadie   I couldn't believe I said it either! And it did mean what he thought it meant.

Joao   We kept flirting every time we saw each other.

Sadie   The flirting got more intense. One night, we were both working late, I said to him (*in a bad English accent*), 'Joao'.

English people hate it when you make fun of their accents. But if you're ever in England they never stop doing it to us.

Joao   I never minded you making fun of my accent but you always did this bizarre nineteenth-century London accent. I'm from fucking Manchester!

Sadie   Ack you all sound the same! See they can give it but they can't take it.

Joao . . .

Joao   That's not even how you pronounce my name. Growing up in England with that name was hard enough but in Belfast? They're all like, '*Jawahwah*'.

Sadie   *Joao* . . .

Joao   See what I mean?

What is it? I'm working!

Sadie   What are you doing for dinner?

Joao   I was just gonna get a McDonald's.

Sadie   Don't get a McDonald's! It's really unhealthy.

Joao   I'm trying to save money.

Sadie   You've got a really good body, you don't want to ruin it with junk food.

Joao   So what do you suggest?

Sadie   Why don't you let me cook you something?

Joao   What here? In the microwave, you mean?

Sadie   I mean come round to mine. For dinner. After work.

Joao   . . . Yeah actually that's uh . . . that would really help me save money. So . . . cool . . .

I couldn't believe it.

Sadie   I couldn't believe it either!

Joao   We didn't have dinner.

Sadie   I don't want to go into the details.

Joao   It was amazing!

Sadie   Just his . . . his stamina

Joao   She was really dirty.

Sadie   Joao!

Joao   You were! Like *really* fucking dirty.

Sadie   Stop telling everybody!

Joao   We did *everything*.

Sadie   That's enough!

All I'll say is having sex with a beautiful twenty-five-year-old after ten years of no sex at all is highly recommended. And highly addictive.

Joao   It was only meant to be for one night.

Sadie   But it was too good.

Joao   So we kept doing it.

Sadie   I used to call him the Duracell Bunny. Because he just kept going.

Joao   And going.

Sadie   And going.

Joao   And going!

Sadie   But if you keep having sex with someone even if you tell yourself it's just sex, you will develop feelings. It's inevitable.

And when I start having feelings, that's when things go wrong.

I pull away.

Scene Three

Sadie *and* **Joao** *in bed.*

Sadie   So I was thinking uh . . .?

Joao   Yeah?

Sadie   Maybe we should stop doing this.

Joao   Yeah I agree.

Sadie   What?

Joao   What?

Sadie   What do you mean you agree?

Joao   Well, it's against the rules.

Sadie   What rules?

Joao   The lockdown rules.

Sadie   But the lockdown's been in place for four months.

Joao   Yeah I know.

Sadie   So why do you only give a fuck about the rules now?

Joao   You were the one who said maybe we should stop.

Sadie   But not because of the lockdown.

Joao   So why do you want to stop?

Sadie   Because this isn't going anywhere. You're too young for me.

Joao   Ok.

Sadie   'Ok'? That's all you've got to say? 'Ok'?

Joao   Well, what does it matter why we're stopping if we both want to stop?

Sadie   Because I don't want to stop because the fucking government says so! I want to stop because we think we should stop. Not because of this unnecessary futile nihilistic lockdown.

Joao   Yeah but if we both agree we're stopping, why does it matter?

Sadie   Do you not fancy me anymore?

Joao   No I do . . . I do.

Sadie   So what's the problem?

Joao   I'm just worried, that's all.

Sadie   About getting Covid?

Joao   No.

Sadie   You're young and healthy, that shouldn't concern you.

Joao   I'm scared of giving Covid to you.

Sadie   Why would you worry about that?

Joao   Well, because you're . . .

Sadie   I'm what?

Joao   You know . . .

Sadie   What?

Joao   Old . . . er. Older.

Sadie   . . . Joao . . .?

Joao   Yeah . . .?

Sadie   You do realise the average age of death from Covid is eighty-two.

Joao   But the older you are the more vulnerable you are.

Sadie   So in your eyes I'm like an eighty-two-year old?

Joao   No! I just . . . I don't want to kill you. That's all.

Sadie   I'm not scared of dying. I welcome death. Death is my closest friend.

Joao   Well, that's a weird thing to say but ok.

Sadie God I despise your generation. Your fear of a disease which is basically harmless to you.

Joao It's not harmless!

Sadie Could you please explain to me why so many of your generation wear masks in the street? When you're outdoors? And miles away from other people?

Joao Because it's a tiny gesture that could save lives.

Sadie It's not a tiny gesture, there's a huge social cost to masks that no one is talking about. They dehumanise us all.

Joao But if it saves one person's life, it's not a lot to ask is it? Look at my nan. She's seventy-five years old.

Sadie You really need to stop saying nan, you sound like a fucking infant.

Joao She's in a vulnerable category.

Sadie She lives in England, you don't even see her!

Joao Yeah but when she does go to Tesco's I don't want her to catch anything from some granny-killer like you.

Sadie This is part of the problem.

Joao What?

Sadie You shouldn't have a granny at your age. Both my grannies were dead by the time I was five. My parents were both dead before I was your age. Your generation is too unaccustomed to death. Hence, the lockdowns, hence the masks, hence the economic destruction, hence the contempt for liberty.

Joao Yeah but my generation has no say in this, do we? It's your generation that are in power, that are making all these decisions. And anyway we just need to wear them for a short time to stop the spread. And then we can stop wearing them when the virus is suppressed. It's not hard to understand. I don't know why you're being so fucking dense about it.

Sadie   But why do you wear it outside?

Joao   Why do you care?

Sadie   I just want to know.

Joao   I like it.

Sadie   You like it? You like being deprived of oxygen?

Joao   I feel cosy with it on.

Sadie   *Cosy?*

Joao   Yeah. I feel safe.

Sadie   You sound like a victim of sexual assault saying, 'I actually liked being raped. At least I got to have a lie-down.'

He gets up and starts getting dressed.

Sadie   Aw, don't be . . . come on . . .

She gets up and goes to him.

Sadie   Come back to bed.

Joao   Get away from me. You're disgusting. Your breath stinks.

She slaps him hard in the face. He's stunned. He exits.

Scene Four

Sadie *is in her kitchen.*

Sadie   I knew it had to end some time.

I went back to my usual lockdown routine. Reading in the morning. A long walk in the afternoon. TV at night.

It was fine.

Only at night time, I got lonely.

I could never sleep.

She takes some more sleeping pills.

But one night he turned up at my door. I invited him in and we had sex again. And I thought that would be it. But he said he was hungry so I offered to make him dinner.

And that's when he told me:

The kitchen. **Joao** *sits while* **Sadie** *cooks.*

Joao   I've started seeing a therapist.

Sadie   Really?

Joao   Yeah.

Sadie   Man or a woman?

Joao   Why does that matter?

Sadie   I suppose it doesn't.

Joao   It's a woman.

Sadie   Do you see her in person?

Joao   It's all done on Zoom.

Sadie   God that's depressing.

Joao   That's actually what we talk about.

Sadie   What?

Joao   Depression.

Sadie   Depression?

Joao   Yeah.

Sadie   Why do you talk about depression?

Joao   Because I'm depressed.

Sadie   Really?

Joao   Yeah.

Sadie   You don't seem depressed.

Joao   I am.

Sadie   Why are you depressed?

Joao   Why is anyone depressed?

Sadie   Well, your therapist should be able to tell you that.

Joao   And that's obviously why I'm seeing her isn't it?

Sadie   Ok.

Joao   We talk about my mother a lot.

Sadie   Do you talk about me?

Joao   Yeah, yeah.

I told her you hit me.

Sadie   What?

Joao   Well, the last time I was here. When I was leaving?

Sadie   Uh-huh?

Joao   You hit me.

Sadie   I slapped you.

Joao   Yeah?

Sadie   I didn't *hit* you, I slapped you.

Joao   A hit is a slap.

Sadie   Yeah but it's not like –

Joao   A hit is a slap.

Sadie   Yeah but you're making it sound like I beat you up.

Joao   No you didn't beat me up. But you did hit me.

Sadie   You're making me sound like an abuser.

Joao   Well, she actually said that.

Sadie   What?

Joao   She said our relationship sounded abusive.

Sadie   Did she?

Joao   Yeah . . . Yeah, she said it was toxic? Abusive . . .

Sadie   Let me tell you something, Joao. This is not an abusive relationship. I've been in plenty of abusive relationships. And this is not one of them.

Joao   I'm just telling you what she said.

Sadie   For a start we haven't been seeing each other long enough for it to become abusive. Yes obviously all relationships over time eventually become abusive. That's the nature of relationships.

She resumes cooking.

Abusive! I'll show her fucking abuse.

Joao   She also said we both had issues with boundaries.

Sadie   'Boundaries'?

Joao   That's what she said.

Sadie   What the fuck are boundaries? What the hell is she talking about? It's all nonsense! *Boundaries*?!

Joao   I think it's like . . . respecting when your partner says no.

Sadie   Is she expensive?

Joao   A hundred quid a session.

Sadie   Jesus.

Joao   She's one of the best in Northern Ireland.

Sadie   That's probably not saying much. What's her name?

Joao   Mairead McDaid.

Sadie   Mairead McDaid?

Joao   Yeah?

Sadie   Are you fucking kidding me?

Joao   Why would I be kidding?

Sadie   Could you find a more Fenian name?

Joao   Oh right. This is a . . .

Sadie   Than Mairead fucking McDaid?!

Joao   It's a Protestant Catholic thing ok.

Sadie   Whereabouts in Belfast is she from?

Joao   She's not from Belfast.

Sadie   So where's she from?

Joao   Derry.

Sadie   Oh fuck off.

Joao   What's wrong with Derry?

Sadie   What's wrong with 'Derry'? It doesn't exist for a start.

Joao   What?

Sadie   There's no such place as Derry. It's called Londonderry.

Joao   She calls it Derry.

Sadie   Oh, she calls it Derry. Mairead McDaid calls it Derry does she? What a fucking surprise! You're English, you should be calling it Londonderry, she's fucking brainwashed you.

Joao   So why do Catholics call it Derry and Protestants call it –

Sadie   I shouldn't have to educate you, Joao, you've been here over a year you should know this by now. Protestants call it Londonderry cos we're right. And Catholics call it Derry cos they're wrong.

Joao   What about *Derry Girls*?

Sadie   What about it?

Joao   Well if it's made by Channel 4 and Channel 4's in England and England's basically Protestant why don't they call it 'Londonderry Girls'?

Sadie   Good fucking question, Joao, and it's your own ignorance which provides the answer. Because you – the English – our cousins and our brothers – used to give a fuck about us. And now you don't.

Joao   Yeah. . . I guess most English people have more important things on their minds than the name of some place they're never gonna visit.

Sadie   You gave a fuck about it four hundred years ago when we were fighting off the Papist hordes on your behalf. It fucking mattered to you then.

Joao   I wasn't around then.

Sadie   Your ancestors were.

Joao   My ancestors were Portuguese.

Silence. **Sadie** *cooks with increased ferocity.*

Joao   I was wondering if you wanted to meet with her.

Sadie   Why?

Joao   I thought we could have some counselling together.

Sadie   No.

Joao   Please, Sadie.

Sadie   I said no! Will you respect my boundaries please?! No!

Joao   Ok.

Sadie   What is going on here? Seriously? You turn up for sex, I'm cooking you dinner. But we're not a couple. So even the fact we're having this conversation is ridiculous. We're just friends. That's it.

Joao   I'd like us to be more than that.

Sadie   More than friends?

Joao   Yeah . . . What do you think?

She turns to look at him. He goes. She turns to the audience in disbelief.

Scene Five

Sadie *takes a seat in* **Mairead***'s office. She continues talking to the audience.*

Sadie   Look, I don't hate Catholics. Ok?

I really don't.

And I don't care if you want to call it Derry. I've never even been there. I get nosebleed when I leave Sandy Row.

But when I'm under attack, the worst comes out of me.

I was touched that he wanted to be more than friends.

Maybe this could be a real relationship after all?

So I agreed to meet her. Mairead McDaid.

But only in person. And only without a mask.

I assumed she'd say no but to my surprise she said yes.

I tried to keep an open mind.

Mairead *enters and sits opposite* **Sadie**. **Joao** *joins them.*

Sadie   I fucking hate therapy.

Mairead   Ok.

Sadie   I think if that's what you've decided to do with your life . . . to pry into people's darkest shit, you might think you're a good person but really you're just nosey. A nosey cunt that relishes the stench of other people's bowels. You're no better than a scatologist. Imagine burying yourself in other people's faeces for a living. It's repulsive.

Mairead   You're very articulate.

Sadie   Is there any reason I shouldn't be?

Mairead   And you're a cleaner?

Sadie   So cleaners can't be articulate? That's pretty fucking patronising.

Mairead   Where were you educated?

Sadie   Deramore.

Mairead   Is that a grammar school?

Sadie   No.

Mairead   So did you fail your eleven-plus?

Sadie   I never expected to pass.

Silence.

Mairead *nods.*

Sadie   Do you know Piers Morgan?

Mairead   I know who he is, yes.

Sadie   Have you ever seen his, uh, *Life Stories*?

Mairead   No.

Sadie   It's a show he has on ITV where he interviews noteworthy people. I hate Piers himself but his guests are usually pretty great. Joan Collins, Burt Reynolds, people like that, you know?

Mairead   Uh-huh?

Sadie   And Michael Parkinson was on it one week and I love Michael Parkinson. I miss Michael Parkinson.

Mairead   I like him too.

Sadie   And Michael Parkinson said to Piers Morgan, 'The best question is the silent nod'.

She nods silently. **Mairead** *nods silently too.*

Sadie   Ok? So I know what you're doing. You're hoping I'll fill the silence. With revelation, with confession. Well, let me tell you this, you'll be waiting a long fucking time for my confession, *Mairead*.

Mairead   I actually wasn't doing the silent nod though I'm familiar with the technique, I was just thinking. You know, what people say the first time they come to see me, the initial interaction can often be the most revealing,

Sadie   Is that so?

Mairead   And you're a cleaner.

Sadie   So you keep saying.

Mairead   Well . . . you deal with people's shit all the time. Don't you? What you accuse me of doing metaphorically for a living, you literally do that. You clean up other people's shit.

Sadie   You think you're better than me?

Mairead   No.

Sadie   You're not better than me.

Mairead   I was just wondering if there was some element of self-loathing at work in what you said.

Sadie   Self-loathing?

Mairead   I get the impression you hate yourself.

Sadie   Everyone hates themselves.

Mairead   Do they?

Sadie   Most people do.

Mairead   I don't.

Sadie   You should. I'd hate myself if I was you.

Mairead   I like myself. And I know lots of people who like themselves.

Sadie   Well, your life sounds fucking splendid.

Mairead   Yeah it's not fucking bad actually.

But you're right, it's common enough in this country. Self-loathing. It's part of the culture of growing up here. The pain, the trauma of our history. You're rolling your eyes but you know what I'm talking about. You're born and bred in Belfast, right?

Sadie   Sandy Row.

Mairead   So you grew up in a working-class Protestant home?

Sadie   Well done for figuring that one out.

Mairead   And you were what, a child in the seventies, a teenager in the eighties?

Sadie   Definitely worth a hundred quid a session this.

Mairead   So you lived through the Troubles? You were a witness to the Troubles?

Sadie   It's like sitting here with Sigmund fucking Freud.

Mairead   You're a product of your environment. Like we all are. And I'm just wondering – who's the real Sadie? Underneath this angry, caustic survivor. Where's the bright articulate little girl who failed her eleven-plus?

Sadie   This is such crap. This is *such – crap*. This was all his idea. I don't even believe in therapy.

Mairead   Good because I can't give you any.

Sadie   What?

Mairead   I'm Joao's therapist not yours.

Sadie   But Joao told me . . .

Joao   Yeah I thought we could have some kind of couples' therapy?

Sadie   You didn't check with her first?

Joao   No I did, I asked her. I asked you about this.

Sadie   Jesus, Joao . . .

Mairead   You did and I thought I told you it wasn't a possibility.

Joao   Maybe I wasn't listening.

Mairead   You and I already have a relationship in place. Sadie, if you were to enter into this dynamic you would likely feel misplaced, distrustful even. It's just not done. But I can recommend another therapist for you.

Sadie   I don't want to go into therapy.

Mairead   Or you could come and see me on your own?

Sadie   I don't want to go into therapy! Jesus Christ! Are you people not meant to be good at listening?

Mairead   While you're here, maybe this would be an opportunity for Joao to talk to you, in a safe space, about the assault.

Sadie   What assault?

Mairead   When you assaulted Joao at your house?

Sadie   Well, it wasn't assault.

Mairead   Joao said you hit him.

Sadie   I slapped him.

Mairead   So you did assault him?

Sadie   It was just a slap, let's not make it more than it was. An occasional slap is part of the excitement of a relationship.

Mairead   Is that your usual experience?

Sadie   Look, I know what you're doing. And I'm not impressed.

Mairead   No I'm genuinely asking. Is that normal for you?

Sadie   Well, I pretty much just said it was, didn't I? Maybe get your ears checked, Mairead.

Mairead   Ok.

Ok.

Joao also said you made a comment about rape that night.

Sadie   Did I?

Mairead   Yes you were having a conversation about masks and you compared him to a sexual assault victim.

Sadie   That was a joke.

Joao   It was very upsetting.

Sadie   He overreacted.

Joao   I did not overreact. I . . . I – I . . .

Mairead   Are you ok?

Joao   Yes. Yes. Yes. Yes.

Mairead   Do you need a moment or . . .?

Joao   No. I want to talk about it.

Sadie   Look. It was a joke. Why can no one take a joke anymore?

Joao   I am a victim of sexual abuse. From childhood.

Sadie   Oh.

Right.

I didn't know.

Joao   I . . . yeah . . . I . . .

Sadie   I wouldn't have said it if I'd known that.

Joao   I was . . . hohhh . . . I was uh . . . when I was a kid . . .
it was – uh . . .

Sadie   You don't have to tell me.

Joao   I want to.

Sadie   Ok.

Joao   When I was nine, I was with my cousin. And he made
me watch . . . uh . . . porn. Two women performing oral sex
on each other. I thought it was disgusting. He laughed at
me. And he uh . . . He got his dick out. And he masturbated.
In front of me.

Silence.

Sadie   And then what?

Joao   Well, that's it.

Sadie   Nothing else happened?

Joao   That was enough.

Sadie   Well, I'm sorry but that's not abuse.

Joao   It is fucking abuse! Of course it's fucking abuse!

Mairead   I think – ahm . . . if I can . . . This is very difficult
for Joao to talk about. You can see that what happened to
him was clearly traumatic for him. And yes it was abuse. To
expose a child to pornography and to masturbate in their
presence? That's abuse.

Sadie   What age was your cousin?

Joao   Fifteen.

Sadie   So he was a minor too.

Mairead   But children can and do abuse other children.
And that doesn't change the fact that the experience was
traumatic for Joao. Can you respect that?

Sadie   Well, not really no.

Mairead   Why not?

Sadie   It's not like he was raped or anything.

Mairead   But it was a violation, Sadie. You can see that, can't you?

Sadie   I think it's typical of his generation to overreact like this. To claim victimhood where none exists

Joao   Oh fuck this. My addiction to pornography can be traced back to that time.

Sadie   All men your age watch porn, don't call it addiction, that's nonsense!

Mairead   Sadie –

Sadie   Well, it is, it's ridiculous!

Joao   Don't dismiss my trauma as nonsense. This is what you do, Sadie! You treat everyone like shit, you trample all over their feelings and then you say, 'Oh it doesn't matter', and I'm fucking sick of it.

Sadie   So why do you want to be in a relationship with me?

Joao   Because I'm in love with you ok?! I fucking love you! FUCK!

He storms off. **Mairead** *follows him.*

Scene Six

Sadie   Well, that was unexpected.

I had to take another pill to get to sleep that night.

She takes a pill.

I didn't know what –

Clark *enters.*

Clark   Is it my bit now?

Sadie   Oh Jesus, Clark –

Clark   It's just I've been waiting ages.

Sadie   I'll let you know when it's your bit! Now will you fuck off please?!

Clark   Alright there's no need to shout at me.

He exits.

Sadie   I took Mairead up on her offer.

And I went to see her alone.

Mairead *re-enters.*

Sadie   I'm sorry for how obnoxious I was when last we met. I felt very threatened by you.

And I'm sorry for the passive aggressive remarks I made about your Catholicism.

I've always envied Catholics their confession.

It can't be good for us as Protestants to carry our sins alone.

It's fine if you actually believe in God, then you can talk directly to him.

But if you're an atheist Prod like me.

How do you deal with guilt?

Mairead   Maybe you go to a therapist?

Sadie   It would be nice to unburden.

Mairead *nods.*

Sadie   You're doing the silent nod again.

Mairead *smiles.* **Sadie** *smiles too.*

Mairead   Why have you decided to come and see me?

Sadie   I feel bad for Joao.

It was thoughtless what I said.

I didn't know he was in love with me.

Mairead   Do you love him?

Sadie   Yes. But I hate him too.

Mairead   Why do you hate him?

Sadie   I'm filled with hate for everyone. I've always been that way.

I'm a cunt.

Mairead   That's not what I see when I look at you.

I see a woman with a big heart. And a ferocious intelligence. Who got dealt a bad hand in life.

Sadie   You told Joao I was toxic.

Mairead   To him you are.

Sadie   Should I end it with him?

Mairead   It's not for me to say.

Sadie   But what do you think?

Mairead   I think it's an unhealthy relationship.

Sadie   I can't stand being alone.

Mairead   You could find someone else.

Sadie   What chance is there of that? Especially this year!

Mairead   It's been a tough year.

Sadie   It's nice to sit here and talk to someone face to face. When I see everybody in masks I feel like I'm being suffocated. I can't breathe.

So I don't go out. Then I get lonely.

Mairead   What do you do when you get lonely?

Sadie   You'll think I'm mad.

Mairead   Tell me.

Sadie   I talk to my uncle.

Mairead   That doesn't sound mad.

Sadie   He's been dead for thirty years.

Mairead   Well, maybe a bit mad.

Sadie *laughs.*

Mairead   What do you say to him?

Sadie   We have a laugh. We talk about politics. Films. Books. He's my best friend. When I was young he looked out for me. Encouraged me. I feel like he's the only man who ever really loved me.

Mairead   Joao said you were married before.

Sadie   To Clark. I see him too. I fight with him. In my head.

Mairead   Is that what your marriage was like? Volatile?

Sadie   Oh yeah.

Mairead   Was he ever violent towards you?

Sadie   Yeah yeah.

But I provoked him. I used to laugh at how thick he was. He didn't like that.

Initially I found his stupidity charming, childlike. But it became wearing.

He died a few years ago, I heard. Surrounded by his wife and step-children.

Mairead   When did you divorce?

Sadie   '92.

Divorce! He just left.

Clark *appears.*

Sadie   Here he is.

Clark   Right, so is it my bit now?

Sadie   Yes it's your bit now.

Clark   It's just you said you'd let me know –

Sadie   I'm letting you know now.

Mairead   Is this him?

Sadie   Yes.

Clark   I'm Clark. 'boutye?

Mairead   Take a seat.

Clark   Thanks. Who's she?

Sadie   This is my therapist. Her name's Mairead.

Clark   Mairead. Ok.

Mairead   We were just talking about your marriage to Sadie.

Clark   Oh aye? What about it?

Mairead   What was it like for you?

Clark   Dunno. We had some laughs didn't we?

Sadie   We did.

Clark   Wasn't all laughs but.

Sadie   No.

Clark   We fought the bit out. But then we'd make up again.

Mairead   Why did you leave in the end?

Clark   Don't want to talk about that.

Mairead   Ok.

Clark   What were you two talking about before I came in?

Sadie   We were talking about you.

Clark   And what were you saying?

Mairead   Sadie was telling me what you were like.

Clark   Uh huh.

I heard you say I was stupid.

Sadie   Yes.

Clark   Why'd you say that?

Sadie   Because you were stupid. You are stupid.

Clark   See what I had to put up with? And then she's moaning about me beating her. She provoked me. I'm not proud of it. But a man can only take so much. My other wife. Married to her fifteen years. Did not hit her once. That's a lie. I did hit her one time. But that was a one-off. She laid down the law, the new wife. So I never did it again. See, if you'd have done that, Sadie, told me not to hit you, maybe things would have been different for us. Maybe we'd still be married the day. Well obviously not cos I'm dead. But you know what I mean. By the way I don't get this.

Mairead   Get what?

Clark   How am I here if I'm dead? Is this the afterlife?

Sadie   No.

Mairead   It's 2020.

Clark   When did I die then?

Sadie   Recently. 2017 I think.

Clark   Fuck.

Right.

See I'm confused.

Sadie   What a surprise.

Clark   I must have been in my sixties when I died.

Sadie   You were.

Clark   But right now I feel about forty-five.

Sadie   You're in my imagination.

Clark   What?

Sadie   You're in my imagination. And in my imagination you're forever forty-five.

Clark   How does that work?

Sadie   You don't know how imagination works? Do you know what imagination is?

Clark   Surely I should have a say in what age I am?

Sadie   No.

Clark   I feel like I should have a say.

Sadie   No! Because for once it's not about you, Clark, it's about me.

Mairead   Is that any clearer?

Clark   I still don't understand how I'm in her imagination but I'm actually here?

Sadie   Oh for fuck's sake, Clark! A child could understand the concept! Are you a child?

Clark   Don't talk to me like that.

Sadie   Stop behaving like a child and I'll stop talking to you like you're a child.

Clark   I am fucking serious, do not talk down to me. Just because I'm not real don't think I won't smash your fucking head off that there wall. Then we'll see how fucking real I am!

Sadie   The point is, Clark, we're trying to have a civilised conversation here and you're undermining me by not understanding a basic conceit. We don't have time for your legendary obstinacy. For your benighted intransigence.

Clark   See, this is what she does. Breaks out the big words to make me feel stupid. And then she wonders why I thump her one. Well, let me ask you this, Sadie. If I'm such a bad guy, how come I didn't tell? Why'd I not tout? Cos I could have done.

Mairead   What's he talking about?

Sadie   Nothing.

Mairead   Remember it's just us here.

Clark   So suddenly I'm not here now? Fuck that. If I'm gonna be here, I'm gonna be here. And by the way, apologise for calling me a bigot.

Sadie   What?

Clark   Earlier the night. You called me an anti-Catholic bigot. You thought I didn't hear you but I did.

Sadie   I don't care if you heard me or not.

Clark   You embarrassed me in front of all these people. There's probably Catholics watching this the night thinking 'Here, he hates me'. Well I don't. I hate no one. Whose is that water?

Mairead   Anyone who wants it.

Clark   Can I have it?

Mairead   Yes.

He picks up a glass of water.

Clark   Apologise for what you said.

Sadie   You did hate Catholics.

Clark   I never hated a Catholic my whole life.

Sadie   You killed Catholics during the Troubles.

Clark   Aye but not because they were Catholics! We were at war. I was defending my country. They were republicans. Suspected republicans.

Sadie   War! Fuck off, Clark! You were no soldier! With your eyesight?

Clark   It was a fucking war! Everyone now accepts it was a war!

Sadie   Not everyone saw it as a war. The cunts who did the killing, they call it a war. The rest of us just thought you were wankers.

Clark   Sure that's the same with all wars.

Sadie   On our first date, you told me you hated Catholics and you couldn't wait to kill one.

Clark   I was a boy! You can't hold that against me. I was a product of the society I grew up in. After I left you, I turned my life around. I became a door-to-door salesman. I sold domestic appliances all over Belfast. Even in Whiterock. So how could I be a bigot? Now I won't deny I was capable of terrible violence. Again but, product of my environment. I used to watch my daddy hit my mummy. My mummy was washing the dishes one time, I was about five, and I saw him stick her head under the water. Honestly. She said something cheeky to him – she was a cheeky fucker like my ma – and he just grabbed her and stuck her head under the water. 'Member I told you that? The water was splashing everywhere. And I was crying so I was. I thought she was gonna die. I thought she was gonna die. By the time I was married, I thought that was normal. I thought that's how you treated women. Open your mouth.

Sadie   What?

Clark   Open your mouth

Sadie   Why?

Mairead   Excuse me.

Clark   Yes?

Mairead   What are you doing?

Clark   What was your name again?

Mairead   Mairead.

Clark   Mairead, that's right. Mairead. Could you do us a favour, Mairead, and keep the fuck out of this?

Open your mouth.

Sadie   Fuck you, Clark.

He grabs her head and pours water down her throat until she starts to choke. **Mairead** *tries to stop him, then* **Joao** *rushes on and pulls* **Clark** *off* **Sadie**.

Clark   Sorry everybody! Sorry! I'm very sorry.

He exits.

Mairead   Do you need a minute?

Sadie   I'm fine.

Red *enters.*

Joao   Can we get you anything?

Sadie   I'm ok. It was my fault anyway. I provoked him.

Mairead   So you deserve this?

Sadie   Any man would do the same.

Joao   I wouldn't

Sadie   Any real man.

Red   She was forever doing this. Provoking poor Clark.

Mairead   Who's this?

Sadie   Pay no heed to him. He's a nobody.

Red   It's true. I never made any mark in life.

Mairead   Who are you?

Red   I'm Sadie's uncle. My name's Red. Not my real name. I was a communist. Back when communism was fashionable.

Joao   Actually communism's quite fashionable again. Mainly because house prices are so high and our generation can't afford mortgages.

Red   You see! Capitalism destroying itself! I could see that coming. Who are you?

Joao   Oh, I'm Sadie's boyfriend.

Red   Ohh, got yourself a wee toy boy have you?

Joao   Actually I don't like the term toy boy.

Red   So what should I call you?

Joao   Joao.

Red   Why?

Joao   Because that's my name.

Mairead   What are you doing here?

Red   Well, I heard a commotion and –

Mairead   I mean why are you part of this story?

Red   I don't know. You'd need to ask her. I'm not real apparently.

Clark *enters with a towel.*

Clark   I brought you a towel.

Sadie *snatches it off him and wipes her face.*

Clark   I'm sorry everyone. I've got a terrible temper but I'm basically a decent fella.

Mairead   Did this happen a lot?

Sadie   Yes.

Clark   Oh I never stopped hitting her.

Sadie   Punching me. Choking me. Throwing me down the stairs.

Clark   I only threw you down the stairs once, don't make a big thing out of it.

Red   But you were a decent type. Let's not forget that.

Joao   Doesn't sound decent to me.

Red   Ack, you wouldn't understand, you're only a young fella. What would you know about throwing a woman down the stairs? Sure you can't even get a mortgage.

Clark   It was a different time.

Red   And Sadie wasn't blameless. You saw it yourself. She was asking for it.

Clark   I don't blame her. I blame myself.

Red   See? A decent type.

Clark   We married too young. Barely knew each other.

Red   And you had your pick of them. You were the finest terrorist in all of Sandy Row. The pride of the UVF.

Mairead   Did you ever kill anyone?

Clark   I did my bit.

Red   And I have no sympathy for the loyalist cause. I myself am a passionate Irish republican. But you have to admire a capacity for violence. You have to!

Without violence where would this island be?

Joao   At peace?

Red   You are at peace. And where's it got you? Sadie told me. You freed yourselves from the Brits only to enslave yourselves to the tiny wee phones.

Sadie   Why are the men doing all the talking?

Red   Sorry, Sadie.

Clark   Sorry, love.

Sadie   This is meant to be my story.

Red   But we're a part of that story. You can't deny it.

Clark   And we're not even real. So you can't complain if we're doing all the talking. We've no agency.

Red   No agency, that's right, Clark.

Mairead   Were you in the UVF, Sadie?

Clark   Sadie? She never believed in anything besides herself.

Mairead   Did you ever suffer any Troubles-related trauma? Did you see anyone killed?

Sadie *is silent.*

Clark   Sadie . . . watch what you say now.

Mairead   What is it?

Clark   Remember, Sadie. Whatever you say, say nothing. Careless talk, you know?

Sadie   I need to tell her.

Clark   Don't.

Mairead   Tell me what?

Sadie   I need to tell someone.

Clark   You're fucking digging your own grave here, sweetheart.

Sadie   I did kill someone.

Mairead   During the Troubles?

Sadie *nods.*

Mairead   Who did you kill?

She points to **Red**.

Red   Who me?

Sadie *nods.*

Red   But I had a heart attack.

Sadie   That was a lie. I killed you.

Clark   But it all has to be understood in its historical context.

Red   You killed me because I was a Catholic?

Clark   A republican.

Red   But I'm family!

Sadie   Not as simple as that.

Red   You dirty Orange bastards.

Clark   Hey.

Red   You murdering loyalist fuckers. It's all coming back to me now.

Clark   Now look, Red –

Red   Get away from me, you black bastard! You're nothing but a lackey of the Queen!

Clark   Now look! You can insult me, you can insult Sadie, but you will not insult Elizabeth the Second. Do you have any idea what that woman's had to put up with? Have you even *seen The Crown*? Betrayal everywhere! From Philip, Margaret, her own mother. And that's just the first season.

Red   What the hell are you talking about?

Joao   *The Crown*. It's on Netflix.

Red   And what the fuck is Netflix?

Joao   It's a streaming service.

Red   And what the fuck is a streaming service?

Joao   It's for watching TV.

Red   Well, how am I meant to have seen that when I've been dead for thirty years. Dead thanks to this pair of filthy Orange bastards!

Clark   I told you to watch your mouth.

Red   Why, what are you gonna do, Clark? Kill me again?!

Clark   You had it coming. You know why you were killed.

He slaps **Red**.

Clark   You hear me?

He slaps him again.

Sadie   Leave him be.

Clark   Stay out of this.

Joao   Come on, mate.

Clark   'Come on mate.' Do you think I'm gonna listen to some wee English prick ordering me about?

Joao   I thought you were a loyalist, I thought you liked the English.

Clark   Nobody likes the English. We just pretend to like youse cos it annoys the Fenians.

Joao   Well, I don't like being English myself but he's slapping an old man.

Sadie   Stay out of it, Joao.

Joao   No! I will not stay out of it. I don't care if you beat me up but I can't just stand by while you abuse an old man. Why do you all have to be so horrible?

Mairead   It's a good question.

No one can answer it.

Clark   Go ahead then. Tell them what happened.

Mairead   Sadie . . .

Sadie   Jesus Christ! All I've had my whole life is people telling me what to do. Why don't you all fuck off? I'll decide what I tell and what I don't tell.

Silence. They all watch her.

Suddenly, **Clark** *and* **Red** *break away and sit on the chairs. They're now in the next scene.*

Clark   Give us another song there, Red.

Red   Pour me another whiskey sure.

Clark *pours* **Red** *a whiskey as* **Joao** *comes up to* **Sadie**.

He goes and sits beside **Mairead** *as* **Sadie** *enters the scene.* **Red**
begins to sing 'The Black Velvet Band'.

Red
  In a neat little town they call Belfast
  Apprenticed to trade I was bound

Joao   I'm here if you need me.

Red
  And many an hour's sweet happiness
  Have I spent in that neat little town

Scene Seven

Sadie's *kitchen in Sandy Row, 1992.*

Sadie *is ironing. She watches the news on a small TV.* **Red** *and*
Clark *are still sitting drinking. Both are fairly drunk.*

Red *continues singing.* **Sadie** *struggles to hear the TV.*

Red
  A sad misfortune came over me
  Which caused me to stray from the land
  Far away from my friends and relations
  Betrayed by the Black Velvet Band

Clark *joins in.*

Clark *and* **Red**
  Her eyes they shone like diamonds
  I thought her the queen of the land

Sadie   Enough singing now.

Red *abruptly stops.*

Clark
   And her hair it hung over her shoulder.

Sadie *slaps* **Clark***'s shoulder. He stops singing.*

Clark   Wha'?

Sadie   I'm trying to watch this.

Clark   Never listen to her, Red. We'll keep singing.

Red   Ah I don't want to annoy your wife.

Clark *leans in to* **Red** *and whispers.*

Clark   It's red fanny time, you know.

Red   What?

Clark   The *bleeding* time.

Red   Oh aye. I see.

They snigger quietly.

Clark   Another Fenian song for us. Go on now.

Red   Alright then . . . what'll I sing? Oh this is a good 'un.

Red *starts to sing 'Whiskey in the Jar', much to* **Clark***'s enjoyment.*

   As I was goin' over the Cork and Kerry mountains
   I met with Captain Farrell and his money he was countin'
   I first produced my pistol and I then –

Sadie *turns the volume up on the TV until it's blaring. It's a news report about the US presidential election (Bush vs Clinton).*

Clark   Jesus Christ, Sadie.

Red *stops singing.*

Clark   Turn it off!

Red   Oh no I want to see this. Did he win?

Sadie   The election's not til next week.

Red   I love that fella. He's the new Jack Kennedy. Another Irishman in the White House!

Clark   Och they all say they're fucking Irish. Fucking Yankee Fenian cunts.

Right turn it down, Sadie.

We've stopped singing now. Turn it down.

She turns it down.

Clark   Sing us another song, Red.

Red   You sing me a song. A good Planter song for my sweet Catholic ears.

Clark   Sure we have no songs.

Red   Oh I know a good Proddy song. A tender beautiful song for you now.

He stands up and starts singing 'The Billy Boys' like an Irish ballad.

> Hellooooo
> Hellooooo
> We are the Billy Boys

Clark *laughs uproariously at this and joins in.*

Red *and* **Clark**
> Hellooooo
> Hellooooo
> You'll know us by our noise.
>
> We're up to our knees in Fenian blood
> Surrender or you'll die
> For we are the Billy, Billy boys

They sing it a second time dancing arm-in-arm around the kitchen. It becomes raucous.

Red *and* **Clark**
> Hellooooo
> Hellooooo
> We are the Billy Boys

Hellooooo
Hellooooo
You'll know us by our noise.
We're up to our knees in Fenian blood
Surrender or you'll die
For we are the Billy, Billy boys

Sadie *stares at them, full of rage.* **Clark** *goes for a third impassioned rendition but* **Red** *nudges him and points at* **Sadie**.

Clark   HELLLLLOOO! HELLLOOOO!

Clark *sees* **Sadie** *and stops.*

Clark   Sorry, love.

Red   Sorry, Sadie. I know you like your news.

Clark   Aye, she likes to keep *abreast* of current events.

He goes to grab her breast. Still staring straight at the TV, she slaps his hand away. On the news, Bill Clinton is talking. **Clark** *watches* **Sadie** *watching Bill Clinton.*

Clark   Do you fancy him?

Sadie *ignores this.*

Clark   Oi!

She looks at **Clark**.

Clark   Do you fancy him?

Sadie   He's alright.

Clark   He's fat.

Sadie   You're fat.

Clark   You're fucking fat.

Sadie *ignores him.*

Red   His wife's a looker. What's she called again, Sadie? The fella that's trying to be president's wife?

Sadie   Hillary Clinton.

Red   Hillary Clintock, that's right.

Clark   They're not Irish with a name like that. Clintock? That's a good Protestant name. Here, that was a crackin' John Wayne picture, do you remember? *McClintock*!

Red   I do remember. And a good picture it was too.

Clark   The Americans hate us Prods. Everyone hates the Prods. We've no one. Why do these cunts all hate us?

Red   . . . aye it's a mystery, right enough . . . Well, let's hope this Clintock fella will be a friend to all of Ireland. Protestant, Catholic and Dissenter!

He raises a glass.

Red   To Clintock!

Clark   To Clintock!

Sadie   It's not Clintock, it's Clinton.

Red   Wha'?

Sadie   It's not Clintock, it's Clinton.

Clark   So why did you tell us he was called Clintock?

Sadie   I didn't.

Clark   We all fucking heard you.

Red   It's no matter, no matter.

Clark   Either way it's a Prod name.

Red   I suppose you're right, Clark.

Clark   Course I'm fucking right.

Red   There she is.

He points to the TV.

Clark   Who's that?

Red   That's his missus. What do you think of her, Clark?

Clark   Aul' blondie?

He screws his eyes up at the TV, examining her carefully.

Clark   Aye, she's alright.

Red   They say she's a feminist. And why not? Women have it hard in America. It's not like here in Ireland where they have the run of the place. It's hard over there for the women.

Clark   I'd give it to her hard.

Red *giggles.*

Clark   I don't like her face much. I'd fuck her up the arse so I wouldn't have to look at her face.

Red *sniggers.*

Red   Aw, Clark boy. You'll get us in trouble.

Clark   Right turn it off now. Sadie. Turn if off now.

She ignores him.

Clark   Sadie. Turn it off. Oi!

She turns it to silent. **Clark** *seems to accept this compromise.*

Clark   What I'm saying too, it's true, the Yanks all say they're Irish. But they mean they're Scotch-Irish. Which is us. The Scottish-Irish. The Ulster-Scots.

Red   Well that's true enough now. Texas, Kentucky, Virginia.

Clark   Aye. Aye!

Red   But Boston and New York are *very* Catholic. Proud Irish Catholic.

Clark   Sure New York's only Jews.

Red   Not only Jews. It's a melting pot.

Clark   I fucking love the Jews. They stick together. Look out for each other. Not like us.

Red   Well, the Jews, like the Irish and the Blacks, have suffered tremendously. But the Indians? Now they've had it worse than anyone.

Clark   Sure what have the Indians ever suffered?

Red   They had everything taken from them. By the cowboys.

Clark   Oh right, the Red Indians. I thought you meant like the Gandhi Indians.

Red   Well the Indians of India had it bad too.

Clark   Ack, everyone's had it bad.

Red   But the Red Indians were completely wiped out. Hardly a man left standing.

Clark   That's the solution.

Red   Mm?

Clark   If you wipe them all out – whoever it is you hate – you don't have to hear them moaning anymore. It's like Hitler. He tried to wipe the Jews out.

Red   He did.

Clark   But he didn't finish the job. If you're gonna wipe someone out, you need to finish the job. Like the cowboys did with the Indians. There's not enough of them around to complain anymore. The Jews are always complaining about what the Germans did to them.

Red   Well you can't really blame them now, Clark, can you?

Clark   I'm not blaming them. you're not listening to me, you're not fucking *listening*!

Red   Go ahead.

Clark   I'm saying that's what *we* need to do.

Red   Who?

Clark   The Prods. We need to wipe you lot out so there's none of you around to moan about being wiped out.

Red   . . . right . . . right . . .

Clark   It's not personal. I'm talking political strategy here. Like one day you're gonna wipe us all out. And then there'll be no more conflict on this island. And that's what'll happen. There's more of you, and you have the whole world on your side. What you have to understand, Red, is . . . it's this. It's . . . *fucking* . . . it's *this*.

Red   What is it, Clark?

Clark   Everything you do, as Catholics, we see it as a kind of genocide. Like when a Fenian and a Prod marry. The Catholic church says the baby has to be raised a Catholic.

Red   Yes?

Clark   That's genocide.

Red   Is it?

Clark   Well, what do you call it?

Red   Baptism.

Clark   Well, it's not. It's genocide.

Red   But if you look back at history, many Protestants wanted rid of the Brits too. Wolfe Tone. Sean O'Casey. Parnell.

Clark   Ack they didn't know any better back then. They'd probably never even met a Fenian.

Red   I believe Protestants and Catholics are brothers. It's all nonsense anyway, all this fighting. Where's it all leading? We're all brothers.

Sadie   And sisters.

Clark   What?

Sadie   Sisters too.

Clark   Ack why do you have to bring women into it? We're not talking about that.

Red   No, fair enough, Clark, women's lib and all that.

Clark   We have to keep Ulster British first. Maintain our precious union. And then we'll talk about women's lib.

Red   No but we have to do right by the women. They're our sisters, like Sadie says. They're our mothers. Our wee girls. Like I always did right by you, Sadie, when you were wee. Isn't that how it was?

Sadie   That's how it was. Yes.

Clark   Right, you go into the parlour now. I'm sick of looking at you.

Sadie   Why don't you go into the parlour, Clark? In fact, why don't you do the ironing? That'd be a nice change wouldn't it?

He stands up. He picks up the basket of clothes and throws it out of the room. They stare at each other – a stand-off. Then **Sadie** *backs down, picks up some stray items of clothing and exits.*

Clark   I wish we could wipe out women.

Red   Ah, we'd miss them now.

Clark   Sing me another of your Fenian songs, boy.

Red   How about a ballad?

Clark   A ballad'll do rightly.

Red   What about 'Carrickfergus'?

Clark   Fucking love it.

Red *starts to sing 'Carrickfergus'.* **Clark** *closes his eyes in reverie.* **Sadie** *appears in the doorway. She watches* **Red** *singing. Then she exits again.*

Red

> I wish I had you in Carrickfergus.
> Only for nights in Ballygrand.

Clark   Oh aye. Oh aye aye aye.

Sadie *comes back in and lifts the ironing board and exits. She almost accidentally hits* **Clark** *in the head.*

Red

> I would swim over –

Clark   Watch where you're going.

Red *is oblivious to this. He continues to sing.* **Clark** *tries to join in at times but he doesn't know the words.*

Red

> – the deepest ocean
> The deepest ocean to be by your side.
> But the sea is wide and I can't swim over
> And neither have I wings to fly

Sadie *re-enters and tidies up more.*

Red

> I wish I could find me a handy boatman
> To ferry me over to my love and die.
> My childhood days bring back sad reflections

As **Red** *reaches the peak of his song,* **Sadie** *removes the iron from its socket and presses it hard into* **Red**'s *face. He screams in agony.* **Clark** *has his eyes closed, drunk and oblivious. He thinks it's* **Red** *singing passionately.* **Sadie** *straddles* **Red** *and pushes the iron into his face again. He screams more.* **Clark** *eventually opens his eyes and comes to* **Red**'s *aid.*

Clark   Jesus Christ, Sadie! What the fuck are you doing?

Sadie   Fuck out of my house with your Fenian songs.

Clark   What the hell are you playing at, girl? Your own uncle!

Sadie   He's no uncle of mine. He's a disgrace to this family. What's he even doing in this house? He supports the IRA!

Clark   He doesn't support the IRA. He's one of the good ones. Tell her, Red.

Red   Aw my fucking face.

Clark *drags him up.*

Clark   Tell her you don't support the IRA.

Red   I don't support the IRA.

Clark   You see?

Red   I hate the IRA. I liked the old IRA. The Officials! I despise all forms of nationalism!

Clark   Are you ok?

Red   Course I'm not ok, I'm in fucking agony! Get me a wet cloth or something.

Clark *does so.*

Clark   I don't know where the cloths are. Where do we keep the cloths?

Sadie *goes to get a cloth. She hands it to* **Clark** *who runs it under a cold water tap.* **Sadie** *and* **Red** *stare at each other.* **Red** *looks fearful.*

Clark   For fuck's sake, Sadie. Over a song?!

Sadie   I hate that 'Carrickfergus' song. What sort of UVF man are you to allow Fenian songs like that to be sung in our house?

Red   It's not a political song, it's a love song.

Clark   It's a traditional Irish love song.

Red   Exactly.

Clark   It's romantic.

Red   That's right.

Clark   And I'm curious about Gaelic culture. Listen. Sing her the last verse.

Red   I don't want to sing it.

Sadie   I don't want to hear it.

Clark   But if you just listen to the words.

Red   I'm in no mood for singing.

Sadie   I don't want to hear that song.

Clark   How is there ever to be peace in this country if we can't even listen to each other's songs?

Red   Jesus, my fucking face.

Clark   Sure we were singing 'The Billy Boys'. And no offence was given or taken.

Red   That's right. And that is a sectarian song.

Clark   No it's not.

Red   I've nothing against it but it is sectarian.

Clark   How is 'The Billy Boys' sectarian?

Red   'Up to the knees in Fenian blood'.

Clark   That's a metaphor. It doesn't mean literally – I don't believe this.

Red   I'm sorry, Clark. I don't know what I'm saying. I'm in pain.

Clark   I'm defending your fucking rebel songs and you're attacking my culture!

Red   I wasn't attacking anyone. Please I just want to go home.

Sadie   Tie him to a chair.

Red   What?

Clark   What?

Sadie   Just do it.

Clark   I'm not tying him to a chair.

Sadie   Just trust me. Please, Clark.

Red   I want to go home.

Clark   Why do you want him tied to a chair?

Sadie   He's a spy.

Clark   What?

Red   I'm a what?

Sadie   He's an IRA spy.

Clark   What are you talking about?

Red   I'm not a spy! Don't be ridiculous. I've known you all your life, Sadie. Since you were in nappies. Why would I be spying on you? Why would you say such a thing?

Sadie   You know your list? In the parlour? The list McKeag gave you?

Clark   Uh-huh.

Sadie   I saw him looking at it tonight.

Clark   I had it secure in my drawer.

Sadie   He was going through the drawers.

Red   No I wasn't.

Sadie   And now it's gone. Go and see.

Red   I don't know anything about a list. She's lying.

Sadie   Why would I lie about this?

Clark   Why, Red?

Red   I don't know but she is.

Sadie   Go and look for it. Tell me if I'm lying.

Red   Clark, please.

Clark *exits*.

Red   Sadie.

Why are you doing this?

Sadie, love. It's me.

I hate the Provos, you know that!

Clark (*off*)   AW FUCK!

Clark *re-enters in a violent rage. He has a gun.*

Clark   It's not there. Where is it?

Red   I don't know. Jesus, don't shoot me.

He hits **Red** *in the nose with the butt of the gun.* **Red** *yelps as blood pours from his nose.*

Clark   Where's the fucking list?

Red   I don't know anything about a list.

He starts to tie **Red** *to the chair.*

Red   Clark, please.

This is insane.

I would never spy on you.

You're like a son to me. The son I never had.

And Sadie.

You're the closest thing I ever had to a daughter.

Please believe me.

Clark   This is a disaster. I better call McKeag. You keep an eye on him.

He hands **Sadie** *the gun.*

Clark *exits.*

Red   Sadie, will you please just let me go? I don't know anything about a list.

Sadie   I know you don't. I've got the list.

She takes the list out of the pocket.

Red   Why are you doing this?

Sadie   You know why.

Red   I don't.

Sadie   Yes you do.

Red   I swear I don't. Whatever it is you think I've done.

Sadie   You know. You *know*. You fucking know. You know.

He bows his head. She points the gun to his groin. She shoots the gun. He roars in agony and falls off the chair. She watches him bleed to death, caught between fear and fascination. **Clark** *comes running in.*

Clark   Aw fuck!

He turns to the audience.

Can I just say I have issues with how this event is being represented?

There's any number of errors here. For a start, I knew who Bill Clinton was. And I never said that about doing Hillary up the doo-dah. I don't like that kind of talk.

Anyway, I'm away here.

Sadie   Don't leave me.

Clark   You'll be alright.

Mairead   Sadie.

Clark *goes to the fridge and lifts out a beer, all the while cheerfully singing the chorus of 'Sally MacLennane' by the Pogues. He opens the beer and takes a swig.* **Sadie** *watches him.*

Mairead   Sadie?

Clark *exits, giving* **Sadie** *a friendly wave and a wink as he goes.*

Mairead   Sadie?

Sadie *snaps out of it.*

Scene Eight

Sadie *and* **Mairead** *alone in* **Mairead***'s office.*

Mairead   Why did you do it?

Sadie   Do what?

Mairead   Set him up like that. Your uncle.

Sadie   I don't know what you mean?

Mairead   With the note?

Sadie   It was a long time ago now. I can't remember.

Mairead   Why did you kill him?

Sadie   I always hated that song. 'Carrickfergus'. He used to make me sing it when I was wee.

Mairead   You killed him over a song?

Sadie   People have been killed for a lot less in this country.

Mairead   Why did you shoot him in the groin?

Sadie   I can't say.

Mairead   Why did you say to him, 'You know. You know'?

Sadie   I can't remember.

Just.

It happened.

That's all.

Mairead   You say that he loved you?

Sadie   Yeah.

Mairead   Did his love ever cross a boundary?

Sadie   I don't know what you mean by a boundary.

Mairead   Was he ever inappropriate with you?

Sadie   He didn't abuse me, if that's what you're asking.

Mairead   That is what I'm asking.

Sadie   Well he didn't.

Mairead   Ok.

Sadie   It wasn't abuse.

It was love.

He was never violent.

I wanted him.

I adored him.

The world might call it abuse.

I don't.

Mairead   Tell me what happened.

Sadie   He loved me.

Mairead   What do you mean by love?

Sadie   Just love. *Love*.

Mairead   Was your relationship sexual?

Sadie   Yes.

Mairead   Ok.

Sadie   That was part of it.

Mairead   What age were you?

Sadie   I was seven.

When it started.

It went on until I was twelve.

Mairead   Ok.

Sadie   It was my fault.

Mairead   Why do you say that?

Sadie   I seduced him.

Mairead   When you were seven?

Sadie   That's right.

Mairead   Sadie. A seven-year-old can't seduce a grown man.

Sadie   I knew you would say that.

Mairead   A child cannot initiate sex with an adult.

Sadie   It happens.

Mairead   That may be how you perceived it at the time –

Sadie   That's how it was.

Mairead   But it's still abuse.

Sadie   It wasn't abuse! He didn't abuse me!

Mairead   So why did you kill him?

Sadie *tries to answer this question. She can't.* **Mairead** *waits.*

Sadie   If he did abuse me, that would mean my whole life has been a mistake. There would be no hope for me. I'd be a victim.

Mairead   A survivor.

Sadie   The world would see me as a victim.

Mairead   It's how you see yourself that matters.

Sadie   I don't want to people to pity me.

Mairead   So what do you want?

Sadie   I want Joao. Where has he gone? He said he'd be here for me.

Mairead   You need to accept it's over.

Sadie   Where is my uncle? Where's Clark?

Mairead   You need to stop talking to your uncle. He's haunted you for too long. Your husband too. It's time to say goodbye to them, Sadie. Stop living in the past.

Sadie   Sometimes I do think what if I were to let the past go. I wonder what would my life look like? Maybe I could meet someone. Or maybe be happy alone. Find some kind of meaning. Contentment. What if there was hope? What would that actually look like?

Mairead   Those are all excellent questions.

Sadie   But what are the answers?

Mairead   I'm afraid our time is up.

Sadie   Ok.

Ok.

Could I make another appointment?

Mairead   No.

Sadie   Why not?

Mairead   There's a bigger problem we haven't addressed.

Sadie   What problem?

Mairead   Sadie.

What makes you think I'm real?

Sadie   What do you mean?

Mairead   Everyone else you speak to is a part of your imagination. So why do you think I'm here now?

Sadie   But you are real.

Mairead   No.

Sadie   You are.

Mairead   No.

Sadie   So, what are you saying, Mairead? You're dead too.

Mairead   No.

Sadie   So what are you saying?

Mairead   How many of those pills have you taken?

Sadie *looks down at the jar.*

Sadie   I thought . . . wait . . .

Mairead   What's the matter?

Sadie   It's empty. Hold on.

Mairead   Are you ok?

Sadie   Where am I?

Mairead   Where do you think you are?

Sadie   Your office.

Mairead   No.

Sadie   No?

Mairead   Think back to the last time you saw me. You told me your ex-husband was violent. You drank some water. You started to choke. You had a panic attack. And then you left. But you never told me about your uncle. You kept that to yourself. Maybe if you'd told me, things could have turned out differently.

Sadie   So where am I really?

Mairead   You're at home. In bed.

Sadie   I'm asleep?

Mairead   Yes.

Sadie   I want to wake up.

Mairead   It's not the kind of sleep you wake up from.

Sadie   Fuck.

So I'm dead?

Mairead *takes the duvet and tucks* **Sadie** *in, like she's a child at bedtime.*

Mairead   Not yet. But it's coming. And sooner than you think

Sadie   Help me.

Mairead   No.

Sadie   Please.

Mairead   I can't. I'm sorry.

Sadie   I don't want to die alone.

Mairead   There are worse things than dying alone.

Sadie   Like what?

A man appears. It's **Red**. *He seems different now. No longer avuncular. More threatening. He sings 'Carrickfergus'.* **Mairead** *exits.*

Scene Nine

Red   You've painted me in a very strange light. You made me into a clown.

Sadie   It makes me more powerful, if I make you a clown. It lessens the terror.

Red   What terror?

Sadie   The terror I used to feel when I would hear you walking down the hall. I would hide under the covers and hope you wouldn't come in.

Red   I was a terrible man when I'd a drink in me.

Sadie   Don't blame the drink. It was you. It was all you.

Red   I thought you were sleeping anyway.

Sadie   I would pretend to sleep when you did it.

Red   I thought if you were sleeping, well where's the harm?

Sadie   There was harm. Oh God there was harm.

Red   If I was to tell you my life story . . . turn you grey.

He sits down on the bed beside her.

Sadie   Don't get into this bed.

Red   Don't be like that.

Sadie   I don't want you here.

Red   I've nowhere else to go.

Sadie   Leave me alone.

Red   I can't.

He touches her.

You're very cold.

Sadie   Don't touch me.

Red   Will I sing a wee song?

Sadie   Don't want your songs.

Red   Why don't you sing a song?

Sadie   I can't sing.

Red   Aye you can.

Sadie   I don't want to.

Red   Aye you do.

Sadie   I hate singing. I have no songs. Songs are for liars.

Red   Open your mouth.

Sadie   No.

Red   Please.

Sadie   No.

No.

No.

No.

No.

Red   Sadie . . .

She opens her mouth. She tries to sing but it's too painful.

A silent scream.

Blackout.